Praise for *Broken Vessels*

"Alyssa is a gifted speaker and writer with a unique voice and perspective. *Broken Vessels* invites the reader to begin the heart work of reframing past experiences and make life changing breakthroughs that reverberate through all your relationships."

—John DeLosSantos, Husband and Best Friend

"*Broken Vessels* is a must-read for anyone who is feeling splintered or shattered. Alyssa's style of bringing her own personal experiences and thoughtful questions woven with scripture makes this study an opportunity to heal."

—Jill C. Dobrowansky, Author of *Faith and Fasting* and Table Talk Co-host

"*Broken Vessels* touches on so many areas in which many of us struggle: seeing brokenness only as loss, turning to things that cannot help us, reluctance to allow time and space for healing."

—Jana Baxter, Bible Teacher

"Through *Broken Vessels*, Alyssa taught me that my worship is most authentic when I acknowledge and use my brokenness. I show up best for others when I share my own struggles, and I'm the best version of who God created me to be when I admit my weakness and let Jesus convert it to freedom."

—Amy Moreland, Worship Leader

"*Broken Vessels* applies to all who have felt broken by their circumstances in life, by words or actions of others, and by their own insecurities. Alyssa's voice, leadership, and personal style shines through as she clearly lays out a path through brokenness to God's purpose."

—Debi Miller, Sowkind Advocate and Giver of Amazing Hugs

"Alyssa's heart is spilled over the pages of this book, as you feel her hold us close and guide us away from the sharp, harsh edges of brokenness, and gently lead us into a tender space of healing and hope."

—Josie Barone, Sowkind Nonprofit Cofounder and Writer

"*Broken Vessels* taught me that brokenness is the beginning, not the end. Through Alyssa's questioning and prompting, you have the opportunity to sit in different spots and ponder. Her writing makes you feel as if she's there waiting on you to be ready to move forward, never rushing, yet always propelling you deeper."

—Lisa Vasquez, Teacher

"Alyssa has a knack for painting beautiful pictures with her words and a kind heart which comes through her writing. Within the pages of *Broken Vessels*, you will find water for your thirsty soul and rest for your tired feet."

—Matt Snellings, Campus Pastor Chase Oaks Church San Antonio

"*Broken Vessels* will help all of us face our own brokenness, so we can be healed by Jesus. Alyssa does a great job leading us in scripture and helping us face our own rough and beautiful stories ushering in the presence of God to do His mighty work!"

—Denalyn Lucado, Prayer Minister

"*Broken Vessels* is exactly what the world needs right now. We are all broken people in a broken world doing our best to act kindly and walk humbly with our God. Alyssa shows us the way to walk in God's grace and mercy throughout the pages of *Broken Vessels*."

—Melanie Shankle, New York Times Bestselling Author and Speaker

BROKEN VESSELS

BROKEN VESSELS

Reframing Brokenness to Advance the Gospel

Alyssa DeLosSantos

ISBN-13: 979-8-9850875-0-5 Print Edition

979-8-9850875-1-2 eBook Edition

Library of Congress Control Number: 2021920758

All Scripture quotations, unless otherwise indicated, are taken from the Holy Bible, New International Version®, NIV®. Copyright ©1973, 1978, 1984, 2011 by Biblica, Inc.™ Used by permission of Zondervan. All rights reserved worldwide. www.zondervan.com The "NIV" and "New International Version" are trademarks registered in the United States Patent and Trademark Office by Biblica, Inc.™

Scripture quotations marked New American Standard Bible (NASB) Copyright ©1960, 1962, 1963, 1968, 1971, 1972, 1973, 1975, 1977, 1995 by The Lockman Foundation, La Habra, CA. All rights reserved. Used by Permission. www.lockman.org.

Excerpt taken from: *The Rest of the Gospel*, Copyright © 2000 by David Gregory Smith. Published by Harvest House Publishers. Eugene, Oregon 97408. www.harvesthousepublishers.com

Excerpt taken from *Altar Ego: Becoming Who God Says You Are* by Craig Groeschel, Copyright © 2013 by Craig Groeschel. Used by permission of Zondervan. www.zondervan.com

Cover design and illustrations by Riki Yarbrough

Book design and editing by Renee Johnsen

For John,
who chose me in brokenness, fought through dark
seasons, and believed wholeness was within reach.
You are behind every line on every page.

For Nathan, Maddy, and Andrew,
whose faces alone provide a reason to turn
back to the fountain of living water. Your
*smiles are **forever** my hope in the dark.*

For Vanessa and Brigette,
who share my story in a way that no one
else can. Your lights always illuminate my
path when I feel lost and afraid.

...to bestow on them a crown of beauty
instead of ashes,
the oil of joy
instead of mourning, and a garment of praise
instead of a spirit of despair.
They will be called oaks of righteousness,
*a planting of the L*ORD *for the display of his splendor.*

Isaiah 61:3

CONTENTS

Y EARS AGO, someone asked my five-year-old nephew what he wanted to be when he grew up. Without hesitation, he answered, "Bigger!" He's been pure sunshine from the start as a blondie with bright blue eyes—and, yes, small for his age. He wanted what seemed unattainable: to be bigger, stronger, taller. He is now a marine and is the strongest, most fit person I know. He got bigger. But not without discipline, effort, and heavy lifting.

Ironically, muscular development happens during recovery. When we weight lift to our physical limit, our muscles actually tear apart on the inside. These micro-tears then modify themselves, becoming stronger than they were before, when we rest and recover.

Being torn apart after and transformed through healing and rest sounds a lot like life to me.

Listen, I am not a huge fan of this formula. I wish there was a path toward growth which does not involve shredding us apart, but the more life I live, the more I see how the heaviest loads produced the greatest growth in me when I have allowed them to.

I am fortunate enough to have known Alyssa for just over six years and count her one of the greatest gifts in my life. She is a bonus mom to my daughters, keeper of my story, gentle truth teller, chief cheerleader, and the sender of hilarious texts. We can communicate in a single emoji and have inside jokes which bring us, and likely only us, to tears of laughter. We have driven the wrong car off a rental car lot, spent hours together in delayed travel, and shared countless tender coffee dates while the busboys clang dishes right next to us. No, really. Every time we're together we choose what looks like a quiet table only to hear sis-boom-bah at some point during our visit. The clanks have become so familiar and comical we don't even flinch; we just lean in closer. Leaning in is exactly what I would suggest anyone in Alyssa's presence do anyway, as she is always sharing wisdom you will want to remember. Her ability to communicate with clarity and truth is unmatched.

Alyssa not only knows the potential for growth and redemption through brokenness, she is a walking testimony. She is ever pursuing insight, personal reflection, and growth even in the hard – especially in the hard. Instead of stuffing past pain away, she is quick to reflect on how old wounds might inform her today.

Alyssa's gift of teaching stretches over the course of a long career in the classroom, as well as in key leadership roles in ministry, teaching bible studies and at numerous retreats. But the truth is, Alyssa is always teaching. Her instruction comes as naturally as water to a lake's shoreline, and just as graceful, too.

The best teachers have an insatiable passion to learn, which runs in Alyssa's DNA. She mines for gold in biblical text with the precision and tenderness of an archaeologist because she really wants to learn—wants to know what it says and why it says it. She brings beautiful insights out of familiar passages through arduous study of cultural context, historical relevance, original language, and her attentive ear to the Holy Spirit's whisper.

While I've learned from Alyssa through wisdom shared in noisy cafés and numerous bible studies, no lesson is as precious as the *Broken Vessels* study you hold in your hands.

Alyssa first shared this study with a group of us in her home. We all came expectant to learn from our favorite teacher—and we most assuredly did. But something extraordinary happened in her cozy living room. Though many of us didn't know one another, we forged a kinship, a safety under the blanket of

Alyssa's gentle leadership and compassion. We reframed the way we looked at our stories and felt safe to share even our weightiest concerns. The warmth in Alyssa's genuine "I know" and "I've been there" beckoned us to unload our fractured pieces into the safest of hands. She led us into a place of rest where the torn apart places inside could heal and even grow stronger than before.

The best teachers believe their students are capable of mastering the material and stretching to the next level. *Broken Vessels* is Alyssa's tangible belief that each of our stories is a redemption story. Whether your muscles burn from life's shredding or your form readily carries you through this season, *Broken Vessels* will transform the way you reflect on your life. The wisdom on these pages offer the beauty of a kaleidoscope view of the fragmented parts of your life and renewed hope for what lies ahead.

Melinda Mattson
Writer
San Antonio, Texas

ACKNOWLEDGMENTS

IF YOU have been around me for any amount of time, you probably know I am the baby of the family. Birth order—mixed with other hard turns in my story—shows up in the form of second-guessing and disqualifying habits. I stop before I start when the prospect of how something will come together feels too hard or too far off. This was absolutely true when it came to getting *Broken Vessels* into print. I wanted to quit a few times because that felt safe and much easier. Without the encouragement and support from a handful of people, this would not be in your hands.

Renee Johnsen, without your belief in my work, this project would still be in a folder on my desktop. You have intentionally spoken love and life into my writing for years. Your voice is the one that cheered for a book when I had not even entertained the idea. Thank you for reading nearly everything I write, for sending texts at just the right time, and for walking this publishing journey with me. You have done an excellent job as my project manager, editor, and chief cheerleader. Thank you for believing I could do better and gently pushing me to go further than I imagined I could go. Your sacrifice for this project is not lost on me. Thank you will never be enough.

John, thank you for loving me just as I am. Thank you for picking me up off the ground when I get lost in my own head and don't see the value in chasing my calling. I am most creative and confident when your voice is blowing wind in my sails. Thank you for printing manuscripts, listening to me babble about content, and lovingly pushing me out of my comfort zone. You are gentle and kind, and I am happy you are mine—forever and ever.

Nathan, Maddy, and Andrew, loving you is the greatest job I have ever had. It is also the most important work I will ever do. You are so encouraging, and I carry your confidence close at heart. Always. In the middle of my brokenness, you were born, and your faces were my portion of hope when I was not sure I had it in me to take another step. Thank you for weighing in on colors and content and caring about the details with me.

To the lovely women in my bible study small group, you are the rarest of gems. You engaged with the content, offered feedback, believed in the process, and carried me in prayer. Thank you for opening your heart to me over the last several years, and loving me as only true friends can do. Thank you for helping make *Broken Vessels* a reality.

Riki Yarborough, you are one of the most talented artists I know. Thank you for partnering with me to create a beautiful cover for this book. Thank you for enduring my innumerable requests for the tiniest of changes until we got it right. Thank you for the sacrifice of your time, but above all, thank you for the gift of your friendship.

Melinda Mattson, your willingness to write the forward was an indescribable gift, but when I read the words you penned, I remembered that your friendship is an even greater gift in my life. You are more than I deserve.

To my parents, you faithfully read and share my work, and you encourage me to pursue my dreams. While there is some requirement to do those things because you are my parents, I know you do them because you truly believe in my work. Thank you for loving me through many broken seasons in my life. Thank you for running in when others ran out. Thank you for suffering through my cranky and angsty seasons—believing that better ones would emerge from the wreckage. Above all, thank you for loving me with the love of the Father and repeatedly pointing me back to him when I lose my way.

INTRODUCTION

I HAVE A SERIOUS OBSESSION with old doors and windows. When this love
affair started, I cannot pinpoint, but it is deeply rooted. My eyes are drawn
to eight-paned windows, old barn doors, and discarded shutters. If any are
within my sight, they are in my hands, and I am examining the paint while
considering all the lovely uses for the once highly esteemed piece.

In their prime, these doors, windows, and shutters were hinged or mounted
and put to good use. They became gatekeepers for cool breezes and ushered in the
songs of crickets on hot summer nights. Sounds of life emerged from thresholds,
and stories were recorded on each pane. One door might hold the story of new
life, while one window became a glimpse into death.

But now, they are discarded artifacts of days and dreams gone by. They have
been unhinged, set aside, and repurposed. These old treasures find homes in
antique stores, junkyards, and flea markets. They lean against fences and are
propped up against yesterday's trash. At first glance, they are not spectacular
and resemble junk more than art.

That is where my love for these treasures ignites—in what has been and what
yet could be. Old doors become headboards, old windows serve as wall decora-
tions, and discarded doorknobs double as clothing hooks. Endless possibilities
emerge in my imagination.

Life feels an awful lot like an old door. We are given specific gifts and talents, and when put to good use, they become vessels for life to happen and hope to flourish. Everything feels great when our hinges are oiled, when the lock on the window functions as intended, and rust has yet to adorn any component. But then, life happens. Hard things like divorce, illness, depression, job loss, and bankruptcy leave us unhinged. We become out of sorts and without direction.

Without faith, my days of feeling broken and discarded would have culminated in hopelessness. Because of the gift of faith, that is not my story. You see, I believe that God has a distinct purpose for my life. I believe the same for you. Our decisions and obedience play a role in how we live out our purpose. Sometimes we suffer a broken pane of glass, and other times we may be completely unhinged. That place—and I believe you know it as well as I do—is where we are repurposed if we choose to surrender.

When I went through a divorce, I felt like a total failure. I was ashamed of my new marital status and all that accompanied the title "single mom." The weight of my own shame was overwhelming, so I could not see a repurposing happening in the middle of that storm.

But God. I love encountering these words in the Bible. While we wrestle to see beauty out of ashes from our earthly perspective, he bears witness to endless possibilities. That is his character. He really does create beautiful things from the ashes of our mistakes, failures, sickness, pain, and screw-ups.

Friend, if you feel unhinged, discarded, or repurposed, I hope you will look for Jesus within the pages of this study. He has not forgotten you. He is not disappointed in you. He knows your broken spaces and does not disqualify you from a life of purpose and mission. He desires to use your story for a greater purpose.

Unfortunately, our tendency is to protect our areas of brokenness. We avoid the work of healing because we are afraid. So, can I speak to fear for a minute? We are good about avoiding painful things because we like to be in control. If we could have coffee and a conversation, I would ask you how that is working for you because it did not work for me. I was exhausted from trying to curate my life, but because my earliest memories felt out of control, it was my instinct to hold it all together. That is both inauthentic and impossible.

Hold nothing back. This work is private and intimate, so lay your hurts and brokenness before him. He is big enough to handle the details of your story. I am living proof.

Broken Vessels was born from a season of layered loss in my life. I found myself face down on my bedroom floor not knowing if I could take another breath on my own. My marriage was falling apart, and it stirred an awakening of childhood trauma. This was the season where the cracks in my vessel gave way to a complete shattering. I needed Jesus like I had never realized before. He sustained me. He extended kindness toward me. He offered healing.

Have you ever heard of the refiner's fire? When a refiner works to extract silver from ore, the process includes heat, at just the right temperature, and oxygen. The steps can be repeated until all the impurities are removed. The refiner knows he has achieved pure silver when it glows.

Think about that process. God is refining us. We have to endure a little heat to burn out the impurities that keep us from pure joy. My favorite part is the added oxygen. When we allow God to breathe life into our broken places, our life light will be so bright people will think it is glowing.

Our lives were meant to tell the story of the hope God offers his children. All his children. Instead of covering up the hard chapters of our lives, we can share the hope we found in the dark. As you study, my prayer is that you allow God to reframe the way you have looked at your losses and challenges. He can flip the script, give you a breakthrough, and restore your hope.

As you walk in healing, your story becomes a window of hope, a light in the darkness, a display of his splendor! May you find true healing as you study.

Alyssa

How to Use This Study

BROKEN VESSELS can be a private, personal journey or completed with a friend or small group. It was written as a six-week study; each week has a chapter to read, five days of reflection, and journal opportunities along the way. If you need to slow things down, you are free to do that.

While the scripture I quote most frequently is from the New International Version (NIV) of the Bible, you may also see references to the New American Standard Bible (NASB). I encourage you to consider the different translations as a way to let the verses come alive and take on richer meaning.

Each day of reflection is intended to provide a time to dig deeper in scripture. The point of digging deeper is to connect the dots throughout the Old and New Testaments, and to provide an opportunity to consider how God might want to reframe things you have held as truth or conviction. There is space provided to write your thoughts directly in the book, but you may also want to grab a journal to record your thoughts.

I want to warn you that this study will require self-reflection. While I know that is not terribly popular in our fast-paced society, when we are willing to open our hands and look at the broken pieces we have carried, we make space for God to work in ways we never expected.

Maybe you are unaware of areas of brokenness because you cannot let yourself go there. Brokenness has a negative connotation for most of us, but where did we learn that? Throughout this study, you will be challenged to see brokenness as a springboard, not a prison sentence.

Healing is within reach. True healing that multiplies hope and breathes new purpose into your days can be found within the pages of this study. Know why? God is near to the broken-hearted, and because scripture does not return void, the effort you put in will carry you to a healing place—a holy place.

Friend, will you commit to really starting before you stop? Give each week a try. If you have to close the book because you are emotionally or physically drained, do it, but don't forget to return to the study. The weeks of study build on one another, so if you stick with it, the big picture will emerge.

Trust the process. When you cannot imagine it getting better, complete another day or week of reflection. Do it for the past you, the current you, and the future you. Your story of healing will become a lighthouse for others.

As you study, I pray God reframes the way you see things, that you will take the opportunity to retrain your responses, that he will give you a breakthrough you did not know to ask for, and that the Good News of the Gospel will reach others as you tell your story.

For additional resources, including a *Broken Vessels* playlist, questions to guide a small group discussion, and graphics to share, visit www.alyssadelossantos.com.

Let's get started!

Week One
Broken Cisterns

Growing up in Illinois, it was common for houses to have storm doors. I vividly remember when my storm door crumbled into a thousand pieces. I was upset with my mother, and whether it was a physical or emotional need I cannot recall, but in my anger, I started banging away at the door. After the fourth time, the glass went flying, and my hand was bleeding. This was a physical representation of what was happening on the inside of my heart. I had pictured my life differently—free from heartbreak and disappointment—but it felt fractured from an early age.

As I picked up the fragments of glass, I was acutely aware that the door would never be what it once was. Holding the pieces would not put the door back together. Its purpose would have to be reimagined. Instead of a storm door, we now had a screen door. The door still served the purpose it was intended to—just in a new capacity.

Broken means fractured, smashed, or splintered. What do you associate with brokenness? Arms? Windows? Marriages? Finances? Hearts? Dreams?

I tend to think of the negative implications of brokenness. Things destroyed or fractured. I grew up in a broken home, and I later walked the road of my own failed marriage. I was left holding shattered dreams and fractured securities, but those very wounds held the potential of healing, hope, and a higher calling with a little repurposing.

If we will reframe our view of brokenness from what is lost to fertile ground for a breakthrough, we will experience healing, and our story—which took so much from us—can be used to advance the gospel.

It is odd to think of brokenness and advancement as companions. We think of broken windows as setbacks, right? Something lost, certainly not something gained. We will discover, as we study, that setbacks may happen temporarily, but in God's economy nothing is wasted. He will redeem the broken pieces because it is his nature to multiply that which is broken.

Consider the miracle of the broken bread that fed "five thousand men, besides women and children," recorded in Matthew 14:13-21. Before provision could be made for many mouths, the bread had to be broken. And to think, the meal would come from a boy, someone who was not even *counted* among the crowd that day. Just as the bread multiplied, God's message of provision and sanctification multiplies when we surrender our own brokenness—the areas where we feel like we no longer count—to him.

It is our brokenness that becomes the conduit of God's grace and provision. Think about the team of disciples Jesus brought together. They were not the perfect-in-appearance Pharisees. Instead, he pieced together a team that ultimately looked like a ragamuffin mosaic. The assembled team was not the number one draft choice for anyone—except Jesus. He accepts whom others dismiss.

Surrendering brokenness feels like a lot of pressure. Pressure is something I tend to avoid. In college, I would drop a class faster than you could spit if the syllabus seemed too hard because counting myself out before ever trying was my instinct. In looking for an easier path, I probably missed the opportunity to be stretched and strengthened by the pressure disguised as hard work.

It is counterintuitive to think of pressure as a benefit, but did you know there are positive benefits of pressure? According to Wolff's Law, a human bone is strengthened under pressure.[1] The more it is put to use, the stronger it becomes. If that is true, why are we sometimes inclined to avoid pressure? The short answer is fear.

Years ago, my youngest child broke his arm playing on the monkey bars. It was the first time, but not the last, that we had to rely on the expertise of an orthopedic doctor who understood the process of how broken bones heal, and the necessity of the cast to temporarily avoid putting pressure on the fractured bone. What I did not anticipate was how my son would respond when the protective cast was removed. The bone was healed, and he was released to normal activity, yet he timidly held his arm close to his chest. He was afraid to use his arm again. Although his arm was weaker, as he used it, it would grow in strength. However, his fear of a future injury rendered his arm useless—in his mind.

Fear has a funny way of dictating our choices. How many broken things do we throw away because, upon first inspection, we render them useless or invaluable? Instead of viewing brokenness as an end, we can reframe the narrative to reveal an opportunity to trust God's provision in the midst of the fear and loss. God will allow our past brokenness to strengthen us, and where we once suffered a break—whether that is a broken heart, relationship, will, or spirit—our strength will return if we allow the site to heal completely.

Hence the cast on an arm, or the hedge of protection around the wounded heart. Protecting the break is simply for the purpose of healing, not to stay on and never be used again.

Have you ever been broken and vowed to never put yourself back in a similar situation? Never love again. Never be vulnerable again. Never trust again. There is danger in that response. Self-sufficiency is often born in such a mindset because it is easy to focus on what we have lost and steel ourselves from any further experience.

When we frame brokenness as a loss or disqualifier, where do we go from there? Leaning into our own understanding, we grasp for reasonable explanations for the hurt. It is a form of coping with pain and loss, and as one who loves a well-articulated explanation, I can get lost in making sense of difficult seasons and miss the opportunity to grow.

God has a specific plan for brokenness, but when we hold tightly to our broken pieces, afraid of revealing our vulnerability, we delay and sometimes reject the opportunity to be healed. Brokenness is a beginning--not an end. The struggle is part of the whole story; it is what makes us human and desperate for God.

Jeremiah, a major prophet in the bible, was commissioned to go and speak to his people (see Jeremiah 1:17). His task was no simple one. Jeremiah 2 is likely his first sermon after being commissioned, and he must deal with one significant issue: *idolatry*. An idol is anything natural to which we give sacred value and power. The people had developed a habit of turning away from God and toward their own way.

In his Growing Christians blog post, Dave Reid shares the following about the historical context of Jeremiah 2:13:

> Jeremiah preached and lived in a day when the people of Judah, the southern portion of the nation of Israel, had turned away from the Living God to do their own thing. No longer were they devoted to the Lord or depending on Him to meet their spiritual needs.[2]

READ JEREMIAH 2:1–13.

Record your observations as you read.

Within the lines of Jeremiah 2:1–13, we see that:

- Self-sufficiency breeds brokenness
- Brokenness results from turning our back on God
- Brokenness requires a posture change: turn back

Self-Sufficiency Breeds Brokenness

Jeremiah 2:5 uses the word "strayed," which means leaving or wandering away from home. This proves to be the Israelites first step toward brokenness. Jeremiah 2:13 culminates with something we are no stranger to.

> My people have committed two sins: They have forsaken me, the spring of living water, and have dug their own cisterns, broken cisterns that cannot hold water.
>
> Jeremiah 2:13

We humans have a propensity to rush ahead and get fed up when things don't go as we'd imagined. We use phrases like "I'll do it my way," "Forget it, I'll just do it myself," and "You can't count on anyone." These phrases and mindset are a result of sin entering our lives. Sin begets self-sufficiency. To be self-sufficient, on whom do you depend?

Thus, we often turn away from God and seek our own way. In his commentary regarding Jeremiah 2:13, Matthew Henry says,

> "My people, whom I have taught and should have ruled, have committed two great evils, ingratitude and folly; they have acted contrary both to their duty and to their interest."
>
> They have affronted their God, by turning their back upon him, as if he were not worthy their notice: They have forsaken me, the fountain of living waters, in whom they have an abundant and constant supply of all the comfort and relief they stand in need of, and have it freely.

There is in him an all-sufficiency of grace and strength; all our springs are in him and our streams from him; to forsake him is, in effect, to deny this. He has been to us a bountiful benefactor, a fountain of living waters, over-flowing, ever-flowing, in the gifts of his favour; to forsake him is to refuse to acknowledge his kindness and to withhold that tribute of love and praise which his kindness calls for.[3]

> What is the result of turning our back on God's kindness?

Brokenness Results from Turning Our Back on God

Notice something with me. The cisterns were always broken, and there is a two-step action here that we are wise to take note of. There is a simultaneous decision to turn from God and turn toward something manufactured by man in Jeremiah 2:13.

"They have forsaken me,
    the spring of living water,
  and have dug their own cisterns,
      broken cisterns that cannot hold water."

Used in this context, cistern is the Hebrew word *bor* (pronounced bore) and means a pit or well where water does not rise naturally but has to be manually filled.[4]

Jerusalem depends mainly upon its cisterns for water, of which almost every private house possesses one or more, excavated in the rock on which the city is built.

The cistern was necessary for survival in the region because there was a scarcity of springs. The point in Jeremiah 2:13 is not the cistern itself; the concern was the pit—also referred to as a grave—that it became for those in Judah. It is our nature to take a good thing to extremes and to be distracted by shiny things. Do not let the parallel get lost on you here. The scarcity of springs in Jerusalem and the reference in this verse to the spring of living water would have resonated with the listeners. It was their inclination, and ours, to be filled up and find satisfaction in artificial things. And the pit reference, well, when we turn away from the spring of living water, sin will destroy us. Only the Living Water sustains us.

Where are you tempted to go to be filled up? Is it your friends, your following, your family, or your job? Sadly, while we spend a lot of time here, these things cannot supply our needs. They will not fill us up. They will not satisfy the thirst in our soul.

Turning away from God toward something else to fulfill what he is and has always been capable of filling will leave us empty and was the real issue. This is the essence of idolatry. We read this in Jeremiah 2:13 and can see how silly it seems, but are we as acute with our vision when we investigate our own lives or walk with the Lord?

In his Growing Christians blog post, Dave Reid asks a poignant question worth contemplating.

> Is it possible that some of God's people today are guilty of the same two evils that the people of Judah committed in Jeremiah's day? Is it possible that we've become so accustomed to the Living Water that we've wandered away from the Fountain to see if there's some water available elsewhere? Have we foolishly gotten involved in constructing our own cisterns?[5]

Here is how I know this is a "yes." When I first came to an understanding of broken cisterns, it was shortly before I was served divorce papers. I sat listening to the words spoken at a conference for women. Phrases I collected during the sessions reverberated within me for days because the Lord was directing my attention to a broken cistern I had crafted.

Because I grew up in a broken family, I had put all my eggs in the basket of doing "family" better for myself. I grew attached to the descriptor and placed all I had into the cistern of a successful family. I went there day after day to discover my worth. Imagine my devastation when that came crashing down.

In his tenderness, God whispered to me "Come to me for all that you need. Let me fill you up and tell you who you are and what you are worth"—because who I thought I was splintered into a thousand pieces.

> This invitation required my response and a posture change.

Brokenness Requires a Posture Change: Turn Back

Where have your seasons of brokenness driven you? Toward self-sufficiency, addiction, work, or depression? God's desire in this passage, and in our lives, is that we would be driven to him because he is the true supplier of all our needs.

Faith requires movement. Movement here is turning back toward God and believing that His provision will sustain us. Unlike broken cisterns, his provision is abundant, unfailing, and satisfying.

> On the last and greatest day of the Feast, Jesus stood and said in a loud voice, "If anyone is thirsty, let him come to me and drink. Whoever believes in me, as the Scripture has said, streams of living water will flow from within him."   John 7:37–38

In his commentary on John, Rodney Whitacre writes, "At this high point of the festival Jesus dramatically cries out loudly (krazo, as in v. 28), If anyone is thirsty, let him come to me and drink (v. 37). If he spoke this invitation during the revelry, he would have to shout just to be heard."[6]

Picture Jesus shouting over all the noise of this crowded festival. *Come to me* [insert your name] *and drink*. His invitation to return to the source that never runs dry echoes over all the competing messages in our lives. Our world is loud and messy, and every time we choose something that will not satisfy, we will find ourselves unfulfilled and longing for something else.

> The longing for God is met with God's invitation to come and be satisfied.

Spring of Living Water

When water rises naturally from below the surface of the ground, we call it a spring. Because of the minerals in spring water, it is considered valuable for its purity and healing properties. It is natural and not manufactured. For anyone who believes, God offers water that is pure and refreshing—where it rises naturally, not manufactured by the wishes of man, but by the generosity of God. Do you see the contrast between broken cisterns and the spring of Living Water?

> "I am the Alpha and the Omega, the Beginning and the End. To the thirsty I will give water without cost from the spring of the water of life".
>
> Revelation 21:6

In Matthew Henry's commentary of Revelation 21, he breaks down the verse as follows:

> God gives his titles, Alpha and Omega, the Beginning and the End, as a pledge for the full performance. Sensual and sinful pleasures are muddy and poisoned waters; and the best earthly comforts are like the scanty supplies of a cistern; when idolized, they become broken cisterns, and yield only vexation. But the joys which Christ imparts are like waters springing from a fountain, pure, refreshing, abundant, and eternal.[7]

Picture the contrast between the waters muddied by our own worldly desires and the water from a spring. When we get heavy rains around here, it is not uncommon to see an increase in potholes. Road crews work their way around the area filling in the holes with asphalt. Have you ever noticed what happens when the next heavy rain comes? The filler washes away, so too it is with us. When we fill our lives with anything other than satisfaction in Jesus, we will discover emptiness when the storms of life hit. Filling our lives with stuff and things looks an awful like the muddied waters of broken cisterns.

Remember when I received divorce papers? That experience initiated a new season as a single mom. After being face down and desperate for hope, God began refreshing my hope, quenching my thirst, and healing my heart. Do you know how God used that to advance the gospel? I found myself sitting in courtrooms with other women walking through their own devastations from broken marriages to custody battles. I bawled my eyes out in prayer with single mothers who felt broken beyond repair. I endeavored to speak the hope of Jesus into seemingly hopeless situations involving lawyers, funerals, judges, and custody hearings.

He uses it, friend, every single part of the story. All of it. It may not be as we had hoped or planned, but we can trust the supplier of all our needs to be who he says he is and do what he says he will do.

Are you satisfied in him? Will you consider taking every need and laying it at his feet today? He is calling out in a loud voice because our world is noisy; his invitation is to turn back to him and turn from the cisterns we have manufactured to fill a need he alone can fill.

When we surrender our brokenness—when we allow him to be the supplier of all our needs—who around you will come into a clearer understanding of what Jesus offers to exchange for our broken pieces?

Aren't you thankful God uses all our broken pieces to create a mosaic of our lives that reflects his inherent beauty?

WEEK ONE REFLECTION

Read the scripture or prompt and answer the questions that follow. Give yourself time to linger in what you are learning because correct answers do not change our lives, but honest ones can.

DAY ONE

Reread Jeremiah 2. We see a distinct turning from and turning to pattern throughout the chapter.

○ Record a few of those you encounter as you read.

○ Can you identify a similar pattern in your own life?

Turning from   Turning to
Faithfulness   ⟶   Worthless Idols

DAY TWO

Read Jeremiah 2:32.

- What area of your life is it easy to forget God?

- What are you prone to accomplish in your own strength? Ask God to restore your trust in this area of your life.

- Invite God, through prayer, to surface any broken cisterns you have crafted.

Day Three

Only God can quench our spiritual thirst. Read the following verses: Isaiah 55:1-2, John 4:10-14, John 6:35, John 7:37-38.

○ Let the words of each verse linger in your mind and then record the invitation each verse offers.

○ What is required of the receiver? Use the insight you gain about the invitation and response to guide a time of personal prayer.

Day Four

Spend today turning from the broken cistern(s) you identified and turning toward back toward God.

o Search scripture for the Truth about the need you have been or are seeking to fill.

o If you are unsure where to begin, start by reading Psalm 139.
Example:
Broken cistern—efforts to be seen because I feel overlooked.
Truth—Psalm 139 says God sees me and knows all about me.

Day Five

Read John 7:37-38 and Matthew 11:28-30.

o Recall a time of brokenness you walked through or are currently walking through. Have you allowed the season to drive you toward or away from Christ?

o Make a list of practical ways he may be inviting you to use your broken season to encourage others with the hope of the gospel. Consider sharing one of the practical steps you feel led to take with a confidant.

JOURNAL OPPORTUNITY _____

Use the space provided to record your thoughts as you go deeper in your study.

o What is God stirring in you? Is there a need have you been trying to fill on your own?

o Where is he pleading with you to return to him?

o How might God use the brokenness in your story for his glory?

WEEK ONE BIBLE VERSES

Matthew 14
Jeremiah 1:17
Jeremiah 2:1-13
John 7:37-38
Revelation 21:6
Jeremiah 2:32
Isaiah 55:1-2
John 4:10-14
John 6:35
Psalm 139
Matthew 11:28-30

Week Two
Lumps of Clay

Broken cisterns are the places where we go or have gone to draw our strength, identity, and hope. Last week, as we studied the pattern of turning away from God and turning toward our own way, we discovered that turning away will always lead us in a different trajectory.

Throughout the week of study, we came to understand that Jesus is referenced as the ongoing supplier of all our needs, and he is the only one capable of quenching our thirst.

Consider the way Rodney Whitacre breaks down the concept of thirst, which we all have, and what we do with it.

> Our need, our thirst, is what we bring to our relationship with God...
> What do we thirst for? What do we really desire? Sin is our seeking
> relief from this thirst in something other than God [idolatry].[8]

We all have a thirst deep within us, and we routinely make decisions about how we will satisfy the longing. In John 7:37, Jesus issues an invitation to come to him to fulfill our need. "If anyone is thirsty, let him come to me and drink."

Have you ever received an invitation? Whether for a wedding, birthday party, retirement, or another celebration, an invitation has an implied expectation from the sender. What is it? That the receiver would accept or decline the invitation. Most of us do not simply open the invitation, admire it, and throw it away. We look at our calendar and let the sender know if we will attend—we *respond* to the invitation.

In the same way, understanding the invitation of Jesus is not the end of our spiritual transaction. He awaits our response. We have the task of deciding if we believe his invitation is good, and then we decide how we will respond.

This week, we will explore God as the Potter and our role as clay. Sounds glamorous, right? Stay with me as we explore this creative concept.

The Work of the Potter

In Jeremiah 18, we see a great analogy describing the Potter and the clay as Jeremiah receives a word from the Lord.

READ JEREMIAH 18:1–4.
Record your observations as you read.

These verses give us a distinct lesson on the wisdom, power, and authority of God. Jeremiah sees the potter working the wheel. The wheel consists of two plates, and the bottom plate would be spun by the potter's hands or feet. This spinning would result in the top plate moving. There, a lump of clay would be placed and worked into whatever the potter intended.

This illustration was for the sake of Jeremiah because he would take this learning into the next chapter. He was learning that God molds, breaks down, and rebuilds. The rebuilding happens as a heart change occurs. Remember, the people of Judah had turned their back on God and toward their own way, and idolatry was a problem. This illustration was a reminder that even when we turn our own way, God, as the Potter, still sits in authority.

I had the privilege of watching a potter work a piece of clay during a spiritual retreat. I was in a large group, and we were instructed to remain silent, watch the potter work, and record our observations. I obliged with tears in my eyes. These are the words I recorded as I watched.

Same piece of clay
Always in the hands of the potter
Different forms
Different purposes
Same material
Stretching, changing
Same clay

Experiences shape us
We can look one way
But with one touch
Or leading we can be
Something completely
Different

Each piece goes through a similar process
Clay must be worked
To become useful
Always in the potter's hands
Always formed just as planned

I found it somewhat frustrating to try to predict what the potter was creating. She would spin the wheel and work the clay, and I would see a vase forming. I sort of delighted, in figuring out what she was creating. Just when my pride swelled like an allergic reaction, she would smash whatever she had created. It shocked me every time. She would continue to work the same piece of clay into a pitcher, only to later smash that one, too. Ultimately, she created a bowl after working the same piece of clay for several minutes.

> The work of the potter is to form the clay. The potter has a vision and process in mind before the clay is worked. If the potter does the work to form the clay, what is the role of the clay?

The Role of the Clay

I took two thoughts away from my observation.

1. She added water to the lump of clay throughout the process. Hold this thought: lump of clay + water becomes a useful vessel.
2. She knew all along what she was going to create—which is a beautiful picture of sovereignty and provision.

> The creator has a vision for what will be created before the work begins.

So, what is the role of water? Living Water is the offer of eternal life, ongoing satisfaction found in relationship with God. It points to the gift of provision we are invited to receive. Consider this equation:

$$\text{lump of clay} + \text{water} + \text{potter's vision} = \text{a useful vessel}$$

The lump of clay is our life, the water is the gift of grace we receive from the Lord, and the potter's vision is God's unique design for our lives. The components together result in a life that is able to be used for a purpose greater than we have the ability to imagine. The clay never tells the Potter what it should become. That decision belongs exclusively to the Potter.

I wonder how much time we have wasted begging to be something other than what we *think* the Potter is creating us to be.

Let the words penned in Isaiah 29:16 and 64:8 ruminate in the secret spaces of your soul.

> You turn things upside down,
>   as if the potter were thought to be like the clay!
> Shall what is formed say to the one who formed it,
>   "You did not make me"?
> Can the pot say to the potter,
>   "You know nothing"?
>
> Isaiah 29:16

> Yet you, LORD, are our Father. We are the clay, you are the potter; we are all the work of your hand.
>
> Isaiah 64:8

In their book, *The Rest of the Gospel*, Dan Stone and David Gregory frame the role of the clay simply in light of the knowledge of Jesus. "Jesus is the Life. He lives in me. I am a vessel, a container of his life, holy and righteous and blameless in his sight. If I know who the life is and where the life is, I am free from trying to become something I was never meant to be."[9]

Think you are beyond usable clay? Let me remind you that Peter was a coward, Rahab was a prostitute, David was an adulterer and murderer, and the Samaritan woman was divorced five times. All of whom were used to advance the gospel message because Jesus looked on them with compassion. He saw beyond their mistakes to their full potential.

> When we can get behind our position as the clay, and acknowledge God as the Potter, we then become aware of our proper posture.

The Proper Posture

We must recognize our position to honor God's. Do you ever feel like we have it backwards—like we are telling the Potter who or what we would like to become? That is a false sense of control, and I am guilty of such irreverence. It seems like I could slide my story right into the book of Jeremiah.

READ JEREMIAH 19:1–5.
Record your observations as you read.

Jeremiah 19 opens with instructions to buy a clay pot, go to the Potsherd Gate, and deliver a message about the problem of idolatry.

READ JEREMIAH 19:10–11, 15b. _____

Record your observations as you read.

Picture the city dump—a place where broken and unused items are discarded. Imagine the sights and smells there. That is where Jeremiah is standing as chapter 19 begins.

Have you ever been to the place where your garbage goes to die? I have one experience taking something to the landfill in our city. As we entered the muddy mess, we were directed to a certain location to unload, and our tires slipped back and forth over the soggy ground. I have never been back.

Landfills are created by carving out a giant space in the ground, protecting the area with a liner, and dumping the garbage in the designated spot. Dirt is then added to bury the waste. This repeated layering happens until a hill emerges where it was once flat. The waste is still there; it is just buried.

We do that with our own lives. We cover things up and keep things hidden to avoid the stinky reality of our decisions or circumstances. We prefer that others see something better than the reality of what is. We are varsity level at prettying up gross realities. In so doing, we fail to present our authentic selves and needs to the world.

Jeremiah goes, as instructed, to the Potsherd Gate to address the people. The backdrop for his message is essentially the city dump where broken potsherds—pieces of earthenware and pottery—garbage, bones of criminals, and remains of children sacrificed to the little "g" god, Molek, have been discarded. A fire was always burning, and the smoke rose continually from the heap. The ambience reflected the nature of the destruction of sin.

What was the message? God, as the Potter, has the power to reshape the nation. Why? They were "stiff-necked and would not listen to my words," according to Jeremiah 19:15b.

These are the same words used in Exodus 32:9. You might remember that Aaron crafted a golden calf while Moses was up on the mountain. Here we see the concept of idolatry repeating. Stiff-necked and poor listeners—does that feel familiar?

I used to remind my students that they had one mouth and two ears, and they should do twice as much listening as talking. We are prone to getting ahead of ourselves and trying to make sense of things. We are wise to humble ourselves and make listening a spiritual discipline.

The verses in Jeremiah serve as an object lesson for us. Truth is, we can chase an idol so far away from God, and when our clay pot breaks, we turn back only to blame God. Although this is not the low position we ought to take, it might lead us to a place of repentance.

In God's wisdom, he created us. Our lives are simply vessels that contain and hold the Living Water we have received. It is not about the vessel, what it looks like or what it was created for; it is about what it contains. Don't miss that.

The notes from my study bible about Jeremiah 18 are rich with insight.

> God has the power over the clay (Judah), and he continues to work with it to make it a useful vessel. But Judah must soon repent, or the clay will harden the wrong way.
>
> As the potter molded or shaped a clay pot on the potter's wheel, defects often appeared. The potter had the power over the clay, to permit the defects to remain or to reshape the pot. Our strategy…to be willing and receptive to God's impact on us. As we yield to God, he begins reshaping us into valuable vessels.
>
> Our society admires assertiveness, independence, and defiance of authority. In a relationship with God these qualities become stubbornness, self-importance, and refusal to listen or change. Left unchecked, stubbornness becomes a way of life hostile to God.[10]

What does a proper posture look like, practically? I think Colossians 3:1–17 gives us a glimpse. Take a minute to read the verses before moving on.

Friend, it is time to humble ourselves. We must trust and believe the work of the Potter, assume our role as the clay, and walk in the proper posture. Our other option does not look or smell so good. Idolatry stunts the gospel advancement, and it causes us to place ourselves above God. That is a dangerous posture.

When we yield our lives to the Lord and surrender the plans we have crafted for ourselves, we will begin to understand that it is not about the vessel—our successes, failures, or abilities. It is not about the size, shape, texture, or look of the vessel. It is not even about how one vessel measures up to another. It *is* about what the vessel contains.

Let us not forget that the only way for a waiting world to see the glory of our Great God is through the illumination of his grace through the very cracks in our vessels—the areas of our lives that were uphill battles, but now demonstrate his faithfulness.

Let us be known to nurture and share the content of our vessels with others. Not just telling others, but living a life that splashes out onto others. Think about this. Would you buy an expensive bottle of wine and hold it up for guests to simply view? *No.* You would pour out the contents and allow others to taste the wine. Right? So too with the Living Water in us; let's share it with others.

> Our humble posture reminds us that our focus
> is on the content over the container.

Say that with me—content over container. God *will* advance the gospel through our lives, the very lumps of clay he fashioned to use to display his glory. May we trust the vision and heart of the Potter, reframe our broken seasons, and experience breakthrough to advance the gospel with the story he is writing through our lives.

Read the scripture or prompt and answer the questions that follow. Give yourself time to linger in what you are learning because correct answers do not change our lives, but honest ones can.

DAY ONE

Read Romans 9:17–24.

o What is Paul emphasizing with this teaching?

o Cross-reference Romans 9:20–21 with Isaiah 29:16, Isaiah 45:9, Jeremiah 18:6, and 2 Timothy 2:20. Write a sentence that summarizes each teaching. How do these verses shape your understanding of the relationship between the Potter and the clay?

Day Two

Read Isaiah 44:1–20.

o What emphasis is made in Isaiah 44:9–11? An idol is anything natural to which we give sacred value and power. Where do you derive security and happiness? Who do you trust? Where do you go for your source of truth?

o What is the struggle and result of idolatry?

o Close by reading 2 Corinthians 10:5, and ask God to reveal any "high thing" in your life.

Day Three

Read Isaiah 44:21–28.

○ Why does Jerusalem need to be restored?

○ Who will do the restoring?

○ What posture is required of those needing restoration?

○ Pray and invite God to show you areas of your life also in need of restoration.

DAY FOUR

Read Psalm 119:57–80 and Hebrews 12:1–13.

o What encourages the posture change in these verses?

o In what specific ways have you experienced God's discipline?

o What is discipline a sign of according to Hebrews 12?

o Turning from idolatry and toward God will prove to be hard work. What will that look like, practically, for you?

Day Five

Read Ephesians 2:1–10.

○ Why would God want us to remember life in our old nature?

○ Ephesians 2:10 refers to us as God's masterpiece. Are you accepting of this title? In his book, *Altar Ego*, Craig Groeschel says, "Chances are good that you are like most of us. You attempt to draw worth or value from the wrong places. You're inclined to believe what others say about you over what God says about you." He goes on to say, "To learn who I am, I've had to learn who I am not. You are not what others think about you. You are not your past. You are not what you did. You are who God says you are."[11] You *are* God's masterpiece. Period. Does the way you carry yourself demonstrate that you believe the great value God has placed on your life?

JOURNAL OPPORTUNITY

Use the space provided to record your thoughts as you go deeper in your study.

o What is God stirring in you this week?

o How are you posturing yourself before the Lord?

o Is there something God is calling you to shift, reframe, or stop altogether?

Week Two Bible Verses

John 7:37
Jeremiah 18:1-4
Isaiah 29:16
Isaiah 64:8
Jeremiah 19:1-5
Jeremiah 19:10-11, 15b
Exodus 32:9
Colossians 3:1-17
Romans 9:17-24
Isaiah 45:9
Jeremiah 18:6
2 Timothy 2:20
Isaiah 44:1-20
2 Corinthians 10:5
Isaiah 44:21-28
Psalm 119:57-80
Hebrews 12:1-13
Ephesians 2:1-10

Week Three
Leave Your Water Jar

IN GOD'S WISDOM, he created us. He is the Potter; we are the clay. He shapes us into vessels for his purposes. Last week, as we considered our posture in the Potter-clay relationship, we recognized our struggle with role reversal in our relationship with the Lord. We explored our proper posture, acknowledged the value of the treasure in our vessel, and considered the view God has of us as his masterpiece.

This week, we will study John 4; the narrative is set around a well and a woman carrying a vessel for water. As we read, keep in mind that the vessel she carries is both literal and metaphorical. It has a distinct purpose to carry water from the well to her house. Metaphorically, the vessel is her life; it represents the need she brings to the encounter with Jesus.

READ JOHN 4:1–42.

Record your observations as you read.

Take note of Jesus' humanity in John 4:6. He was tired from the journey and opted to sit down by a well. Hold that in your mind. Jesus, being fully God and man, illustrates for us where to go when we thirst. He sets himself up at a well as if to point an arrow directly to the message that he offers living water that quenches physical and spiritual thirst.

He stops at an extremely hot time of day—the sixth hour—which would have been noon. Not only did he have a physical thirst, but he was a living illustration of his invitation to us.

Bring Your Need

The Samaritan woman, whose name we do not learn, comes to the well out of need. She brings her vessel with the intention of drawing water to sustain her basic needs. The fact that she comes at this hour is of peculiar nature because women would have come in the early hours before the sun was high or in the evening. This implies that she was not in active community with the women in her village. Her history defined her. Whether it was her shame or humiliation, she still came to the well because her need did not change—though her social standing did. It is worth noting that she knew where to take her need for water. She did not go to the well seeking conversation or companionship; she went with a physical need, but what she found was an unanticipated opportunity to engage a suppressed personal need.

Engage in Conversation

Jesus begins the conversation in John 4:7 by asking, "Will you give me a drink?" She is caught off guard with the interaction, so she carries on guarded. We, too, carry ourselves guarded when we are broken, scared, or unwilling to trust.

John 4:9 points out an obstacle for her in fulfilling Jesus' request for water. She emphasizes that Jews and Samaritans do not use vessels in common. Picture the vessel she carried in her arms. It was created to hold something. If the vessel is empty, is it really fulfilling its purpose? She poses a cultural question, and Jesus takes the conversation to a new level by shifting from the tangible water to the eternal life he offers.

> How often do we hesitate to engage with Jesus because of excuses? What restoration have we missed because we automatically disqualified ourselves?

The conversation hits a crescendo in John 4:15, and she asks for the water He's offering. In a sermon posted on the Keep Believing Ministries website, the following commentary gives profound insight into this unexpected encounter.

> He is tired and thirsty, and she has the water he needs. But he has the water she needs. He was thirsty and knew it. She was thirsty and didn't know it. The woman did not come to the well seeking Christ, but he came to the well seeking her. In his approach we see the great heart of our Lord Jesus is without prejudice. It matters not to him that others would not go to Samaria and others would not speak to this woman. He welcomes all and shuns none.[12]

Be Honest about What is Broken

John 4:16–17 reveals how the conversation turns. Suddenly, although she has pushed through the cultural and gender issues the conversation presents, she is faced with a social issue. She is a broken woman, and the words Jesus utters surely elicit a sinking feeling in her gut.

> "Go, call your husband and come back."
> "I have no husband," she replied.

She could have said 101 things. She could have saved face, if you will, said OK, and never looked back. It's worth noting that she was honest. She knew that her story was obvious to others, but she took it a step further and surrendered it to Jesus even though it was humiliating and uncomfortable. It had, after all, previously brought condemnation. Like her, we are inclined to protect our hurts—but at what cost?

READ THE RESPONSE OF JESUS IN JOHN 4:17–18.
Record your observations as you read.

Do you detect anything but gentleness in the conversation at the well? Her honesty positioned her to be free to receive the gift Jesus was offering.

The conversation between Jesus and the Samaritan woman is both the longest recorded exchange Jesus had in scripture, and it is the first self-confession of his deity. Jesus revealed this in John 4:26 when he says, "I, the one speaking to you—I am he." The woman—whose name we don't know—is the first person to hear Jesus declare his divine nature as both God and man.

This is no chance encounter. Her brokenness had skewed her identity. She carried a label with her everywhere she went, and if she ever had a moment of memory-lapse, you can be sure the community kept score and reminded her. The power of this encounter is that it flipped the script on the context of her identity.

> She could not know who she was until she knew who he was.

The magnitude of grace and provision is never more evident than in this moment. The contrast of her brokenness and Jesus' mercy should not be lost on us.

Her honesty yields unexpected results; it birthed a breakthrough of epic proportions. Just look at the ripple of her decision. Her life was undeniably different. Her breakthrough influenced others. Jesus wants that from us and for us, too. We are welcome to take our needs into conversation with him and be honest. When we are poured out, he can fill our vessels with exactly what we need and remind us of our true identity.

Years ago, we watched the most riveting skit at John 3:16 Live. A woman playing a young girl carried a duffel bag around on her shoulder as she went through her day. She collected rocks with each negative interaction and placed them in her bag. It was a powerful display of how innate it is for us to carry around labels of failures and weaknesses. At one point, when the bag was clearly a burden to the young girl, my daughter leaned over and whispered a message that seared in my mind. She said, "She doesn't have to carry that around. She can just set the bag down." She was so right. It sounds so simple, but in that moment, I realized how inclined I was to carry the heavy burden of all my mistakes and failures.

"Setting it down" is what happened with the woman at the well.

Leave Your Water Jar

John 4:28 is easily one of my favorite lines in this narrative. She left her vessel at the well. Again, this is literal and symbolic. What she carried to the well, she left there. If our vessel is, in essence, our very lives, why would leaving it at the well make sense? We don't have to continue filling our lives with what we think we need: activities, volunteering, hustling, successes, elaborate vacations, or thousands of followers on social media. We offer our lives to the Lord and invite him to fill us with himself. Are you running on empty? Are you exhausted trying to meet all your needs? You can leave your water jar and let your vessel fill up with the Living Water.

> Leaving the water jar and being filled with the Living Water will set your feet on a new mission.

Become a Missionary to Your Own People

John 4:39–42 challenges us to consider what God will do if we

- Bring our need
- Engage in conversation
- Are honest about our brokenness
- Leave our water jar—our very lives

Our brokenness, and subsequent encounter with Jesus, becomes a powerful testimony. If we are willing to open our mouths and share our story, people come to know the saving power of Jesus. She did not boast in herself; she remained humble and invited people to go and see for themselves. She pointed others toward Jesus. As a result, according to John 4:41 , "many more became believers."

This is our commission, too. We are invited to use our lives, vessels designed by God and filled with his Spirit, to point those around us to Jesus. Maybe you are slaying that task. Maybe you are not. Here is what we must take away from this lesson: God desires to use vessels. Not perfect vessels, mind you, but surrendered ones. Yes, even cracked ones. Let's stop trying to repair our vessel, hide the imperfections, or see our lives as unusable.

Consider this. The Beatles were told they had no future as a band. Walt Disney was told he lacked imagination—of all things. Oprah was told she was unfit for TV. What if they had let those labels define or sideline them?

What if we became people who were willing to let God use the cracks in our vessels for his glory? Like the Samaritan woman's experience in John 4, how might our willingness be fertile soil for the advancement of the gospel? Who are your people that need to see his light radiate through your fragmented story?

There is an old fable from China that lends itself to this very concept. It reads like this:

> Once upon a time there was an elderly Chinese woman who owned two large clay pots. She would hang each pot on the ends of a pole which she carried across her neck. Each day she would walk from her house to the nearby stream to fetch water. She would fill up both pots, pick up the pole and walk back to her house. One of the pots had a crack in it while the other pot was perfect and always delivered a full pot of water. At the end of the long walk back to her house, the cracked pot always arrived only half full. Because of the crack, half the water had leaked out during the trek.
>
> For two full years, this happened daily. The Chinese woman arrived home with only one and a half pots of water. Of course, the perfect pot was proud that it had never lost a drop of precious water. But the poor cracked pot was ashamed of its imperfection and was miserable. The cracked pot thought of itself as a complete failure. One day, the cracked pot was so tired of failing that it spoke to the woman. The cracked pot

said, "I am ashamed of myself because this crack in my side causes water to leak out all the way back to your house. I have failed you, and I'm sorry. Maybe you need to replace me with another pot that isn't cracked."

The old woman smiled and said gently, "Did you notice that there are flowers on your side of the path, but not on the other pot's side? I have always known about your flaw, so I planted flower seeds on your side. And every day as I've walked back you've been watering those seeds. For the past two years I've been able to pick the flowers to decorate my table. Without you being just the way you are, there would have been no beautiful flowers to grace my home."[13]

Trials can define or refine us. We get to choose. Refining is rough but choosing to be defined by our brokenness can be detrimental. It is high time we surrender painful words, the opinions of others, and past indiscretions at the well and drink deeply from the Living Water. When we surrender our fears and failures, sit open-handed before God, and believe, we will find ourselves filled up with the Spirit. We become less dependent on our performance and success and more confident in what God will do through the cracks in our stories. There—steeped in honesty and new identity—our lives assume a new trajectory and mission.

WEEK THREE REFLECTION

Read the scripture or prompt and answer the questions that follow. Give yourself time to linger in what you are learning because correct answers do not change our lives, but honest ones can.

DAY ONE

Read John 4:1–42.

o What strikes you about the story of the woman at the well?

o Where does her story intersect with yours?

o What breakthrough—epiphany or resolution of a current or previous struggle—does she have in this encounter? Describe the shift in her actions.

o Is there anything you have been carrying that you need to surrender?

DAY TWO

Read Matthew 9:18–26 and Mark 5:24–34. Today's reading introduces us to another broken woman who encountered Jesus.

○ What is the woman's brokenness, and what does it drive her to do?

○ Where was the woman when she encountered Jesus?

○ Where did she take her need? Where are you inclined to take yours?

○ What is the significance of Jesus' response in Mark 5:32-34?

DAY THREE

The InterVarsity Press commentary on the account of the woman from Matthew 9 and Mark 5 explains, "Desperation has driven many of us to a faith that refuses to be deterred. This woman was undoubtedly more desperate than most of us have been, and she pressed her way to Jesus with the determination of faith, regardless of the consequences."[14] This woman had long been pushed aside because of her bleeding issue, but we see her choose to push through obstacles in Mark 5. Read Leviticus 15:25–30.

○ What made her move, in Mark 5, so risky?

○ What was likely the cause of her delay (waiting 12 years)?

○ Do you ever delay surrendering to Jesus for fear of being exposed? Explain.

○ Pray and ask Jesus if there is something in your life you have pushed aside that he is calling you to "push through."

DAY FOUR

Reread Mark 5:24–34. Notice how the woman's healing came in the middle of a very crowded area? Linger in that thought for a few minutes.

o What might the significance be of where she was healed?

o Why might healing happen in a crowd? How would this facilitate the advancement of the gospel?

o How would the watching crowd be impacted by what they witnessed? What power do you think her testimony had after this interaction?

DAY FIVE

Jesus called the woman "daughter" in Mark 5:34. This was the only time he did so in scripture.

o What does that teach you about how he received her surrender?

o She was a broken vessel, but healing came when she told him the whole truth (Mark 5:33). What heals her (verse 34)?

o Is Jesus stirring you to surrender something specific? Close the day surrendering the whole truth to Jesus. Tell him where you are suffering or where you feel inadequate. He is clean enough for our uncleanliness.

Use the space provided to record your thoughts as you go deeper in your study.

○ Did you know that a starfish can regenerate? If one of the arms of a starfish breaks off, and the starfish is returned to the water source, the broken limb will regrow. This is true for us, too. *We* do not have to hold on to the broken pieces; we can surrender them to God, but we also must return to the Living Water—the source for believers.

○ Do you sense him inviting you to the well? What need does he want to meet?

○ Are you willing to let go of the broken pieces in your hands? Write out your thoughts or declare your decision to let go of the story that broke you.

Week Three Bible Verses

John 4:1-42
Matthew 9:18-26
Mark 5:24-34
Leviticus 15:25-30

Week Four
Shine On

GOD DESIRES to use our stories to reveal his goodness. When we are honest about what is broken and engage with the truth of what we really need, we discover fertile soil for sharing our testimony of who we once were and who we are yet becoming. Last week, we spent time exploring how important it is to give our lives as a vessel to the mission of the gospel. We discovered that taking our needs to Jesus and trusting him with the whole truth, a total surrender of ourselves, births healing. It's not our commission to tend to our brokenness and then present ourselves as pleasing sacrifices. We are invited to bring all the broken, unclean areas and present them to our Father—just as we are. Why? Because he is clean enough for all of us.

So, what makes this process so difficult? Why do we have to repeat this lesson over and over? Why do we insist on taking the field trip and not learn the lesson in the proverbial classroom? Pushing hard things aside is easier in the moment; it gives us temporary relief, but it complicates long-term results. How many times have we been guilty of "waiting until later" without ever making a conscious plan for later? The woman in Mark 5:24–34 had tried everything on her own, but when she took a risk and carried her need to Jesus—pushing through the crowd—she was healed.

We are inclined to push aside what we may need to push through. We try to fix and clean up instead of carrying the brokenness to Jesus.

This week we are going to dive into several scriptures to see what we can learn about the purpose and calling we have as a vessel. To do that, let's take a trip down memory lane.

Remember our Origin

Spoiler alert: There is an implied faith in the discussion of our origin. Based on a belief that God is the Creator, and we are the creation. Let's go way back to the beginning of the Old Testament and look at Genesis 2 to remember our roots. This immediately follows the creation narrative where we see that the Creator looks at what he has created and rests.

God saw all that he had made, and it was very good.

Genesis 1:31

READ GENESIS 2:1–22.

Record your observations as you read.

Then the LORD God formed the man of dust from the ground, and breathed into his nostrils the breath of life; and the man became a living person.

Genesis 2:7 NASB

If Eve was formed from Adam's rib, what did God use to form Adam? Dust of the ground according to the New Living Translation and the New International Version. Our origin is from dust and in Genesis 3:19, after Adam and Eve have eaten of the forbidden fruit, God tells them that they are from dust and to dust they will return. This is a direct reference to Genesis 2:7, so what is the point we need to take away from these two verses?

Ordinary Vessels

We are ordinary, and we live in a world where that is not a popular term. Ordinary means normal, common, standard, or typical. Somehow, we would rather not have those words describe our relationships, our talents, our children, our work, or our accomplishments. But our acceptance of being ordinary, earthen vessels or containers, underscores that life begins when God breathes into us, *not* when we do enough good deeds, memorize the correct amount of scripture, heal from past trauma, or are well-liked.

We are frequently referred to as jars of clay in scripture. There is a close affiliation between the idea of being clay and the reference to earthenware. Can you see it? These immortal bodies we walk around in are clay pots, ordinary containers, but it was never supposed to be about the container. This concept is what I call "content over container" theology.

Adam remained a shell of a body until God breathed in him the breath of life. Then, according to Genesis 2:7, the man became a living person.

There is nothing terribly fancy about how our bodies were formed. The point is to remember that we are lifeless shells until God brings us to life. What is it, according to the scripture, that brings life?

God's Breath Brings Life

If our life is given to us by the breath of God, then it is fair to say that our life and worth come from God's Spirit. Period. How many of us suffer fatigue from trying to be enough, achieve enough, have enough friends, or do good enough? When we focus on ourselves, we are—in essence—turning away from God and turning toward a broken cistern. We then give a lot of attention to our containers instead of the gift of the Spirit that we have been given—the content of our containers.

Is this idea of breath and breathing familiar?

READ JOHN 20:19–22.
Record your observations as you read.

Jesus appears to the disciples following his resurrection. They are afraid and hiding behind locked doors when he arrives. He then breathes on them and says, "Receive the Holy Spirit" (John 20:22).

God's breath brings life, and God's breath through Jesus gives the deposit of the Holy Spirit. This interaction with the disciples points back to what we have already studied in John 7:37–39; Jesus, in a loud voice, invites the crowd to come to him for living water. Now we see this fulfilled as Jesus breathes onto the disciples.

Let's circle back to Genesis and the story of Adam, the first man. Did you know that Jesus has been referred to as the second Adam. Stay with me for just a second.

Read 1 Corinthians 15:45–48. According to verse 45, Adam became a living being, but Jesus was a life-giving spirit. While Adam was born from the dust, Jesus was born from heaven. While Adam was the beginning of mankind, Jesus would redeem mankind.

Because Jesus was without sin, he was able to restore that which sin divided and had broken. "And having been perfected, He became the source of eternal salvation for all those who obey Him" (Hebrews 5:9 NASB). This is the hope we have in Christ.

> Because he came, we don't have to stay broken and ordinary.

Treasures IN, Shine Out

READ 2 CORINTHIANS 4:1–10.

Record your observations as you read.

The treasure is not the *jar* of clay. The treasure, according to 2 Corinthians 4:7, is *in* the jar of clay. Haven't we seen this unfold with the scriptures we've already studied? We were created from the earth, hence the reference to the jar of clay, and nothing happened to us until God breathed life into us. And now we have the gift of the Holy Spirit to empower us to carry out our calling here on earth.

So what is it we are to fulfill? Let's go back to 2 Corinthians 4:1–10. Read the verses and listen for any word or concept you hear repeating.

Did you hear it? Light. The point here is that our lives—including our countless errors and flaws—are vessels that house the greatest treasure we could ever receive. The inappropriateness, or contrast, between the jar and the treasure is intended. Why?

We would be tempted to become prideful, maybe. We might forget we are weak on our own. We might stunt our spiritual growth by failing to be in daily contact with God through our study of the Word and prayer. Maybe it's because of our nature to make ourselves idols. Maybe it is because God knew our tendency toward idolatry, exalting objects above him.

Let's return to Adam for a second. In Genesis 3, we read the account of Adam and Eve eating from the tree of the knowledge of good and evil. This tiny act of rebellion put distance between Adam and God, which translated to sin that continues to separate us from God. Why? Because Adam decided to act on his own, and there in that moment, idolatry enters the picture. The rest of the narrative of the Bible reveals the great length God went to fill the gap sin created.

We have been entrusted with the salvation message of the gospel. *The treasure is in us.* God's intent has always been to use his people to spread the Good News of the free gift of forgiveness he extends. When we tell our stories, people see God through the cracks of our ordinary vessels. Ordinary, friend. We aren't supposed to be the big deal; he is. The big deal is supposed to be the hope and grace that shines out of the cracks.

> Our brokenness is not our identity, but it becomes our ministry!
> We have to loosen the grip we have on our mistakes.

I had a favorite wine glass. It was a treasure that I brought home from my 40th birthday weekend in Nashville. It was stemless and boasted an Arrington Vineyards emblem. *Swoon.* Imagine my true sadness when I witnessed it shatter into a million pieces. My breath caught in my throat, and I steeled myself against the tears that wanted to well up. It was just a glass, after all. A few days later, as I traipsed barefoot through the kitchen, I was stopped by a sharp pain in my heel. Although I could not see anything, the pain was pulsating. I hobbled to my bathroom, turned on all the lights, howled and fussed like a toddler, and then I saw the shard of glass. Gathering up the tweezers and laboring for several minutes, I was able to get it out.

It struck me how much this is like our lives. We are ordinary containers, which was always God's intention, but when we are broken and cling to him for healing and salvation, he spills out of us and onto others. Others are influenced and affected by the shattered pieces of our stories. The fractures and cracks are what allow the brightness of our light to radiate out. This is why brokenness allows the gospel to advance.

In her article on Crosswalk.com, Debbie McDaniel writes, "The scars of life, the healed wounds, the deep lines, they all have stories to tell. Yet often we try to hide them away, preferring instead to present to the world, a safe façade of who we are, a more 'perfect' version."[15]

I do not want to do that. I do it, but I don't want to. I want to be a woman who allows the story of God's healing and grace to emerge from the cracks in her vessel. Why are we so inclined to only share the perfect version?

In 2 Corinthians 12:9-12 Paul, referencing a thorn—something causing him discomfort—points to the purpose of our imperfections.

> But he said to me, "My grace is sufficient for you, for my power is made perfect in weakness." Therefore I will boast all the more gladly about my weaknesses, so that Christ's power may rest on me. That is why, for Christ's sake, I delight in weaknesses, in insults, in hardships, in persecutions, in difficulties. For when I am weak, then I am strong.

The cracks in our stories become a point of reference for God to make himself evident to those around us if we believe his power is made perfect in that space. We give too much thought to what others will think about us, and we miss the point of what others might think about God through the very thing that makes us insecure.

> Can you imagine what might happen if we allowed the light to shine out of the cracks and not just cover it up for fear of what others might think?

What if the woman at the well simply treasured her encounter with Jesus in her heart? Think of the number of witnesses in the crowd the day the woman with the issue of blood reached for Jesus. What if the boy who wasn't counted among the 5,000 just kept his fish and bread to himself?

Someone is watching. Someone is desperate for hope. Many need Jesus. You have influence. You have opportunities in front of you. Be radiant for him. Allow the Good News of your salvation, both your rescue and restoration, to ooze out of the cracks.

"I used to pray that God would feed the hungry, or do this or that, but now I pray that he will guide me to do whatever I'm supposed to do, what I can do. I used to pray for answers, but now I'm praying for strength. I used to believe that prayer changes things, but now I know that prayer changes us and we change things."[16]

Mother Teresa

If you have accepted Christ, the treasure of the Holy Spirit is in you. You do not have to clean up the container or hide the parts of your story that caused you to break. I know it is difficult to believe, but the intersection of your brokenness and healing is both your ministry and radiance.

Will you let your light shine?

Read the scripture or prompt and answer the questions that follow. Give yourself time to linger in what you are learning because correct answers do not change our lives, but honest ones can.

Day One

Read 2 Timothy 2:20–21 and 2 Timothy 3:14–17.

o What is required of us to be used to the fullest potential?

o According to 2 Timothy 3, how do we keep ourselves pure?

o Glance back at 2 Timothy 1:5–11. Where does Paul say Timothy's faith originated? What implication does this have for you?

o How does 2 Timothy 1:7–8 challenge you to allow the Light of Christ to emanate from your vessel?

Day Two

Read Hebrews 11:1–6.

○ What is faith?

○ Where have you walked in faith? What situation have you recently walked through where you had to hold tightly to faith?

○ Read Hebrews 11:7–10. What word is used to describe Noah and Abraham? What connection can you assume between faith and obedience? Explain.

○ What role does obedience play in the spreading of the gospel? What has or might that look like in your life?

Day Three

Read Matthew 14:13–21.

o What was the need? Where did the disciples take the need?

o What was the solution offered by the disciples? How did that compare with Jesus' solution?

o In what ways do you identify with the disciple's reaction?

o Reread Matthew 14:18–19. What is the order of events in this section? What did the disciples do first? What did Jesus do next?

o Reflect on the correlation between the broken bread and the provision of food?

Day Four

Read Matthew 14:18–19 and Matthew 26:26–30.

○ In these two accounts, we see something broken and something multiplied and given. In the earlier account, what is multiplied? In the account of the Last Supper, what was given?

○ How is the earlier account a foreshadowing of the latter account?

○ What has God broken in you to bring forth a multiplication?

Day Five

Review the scriptures we explored this week. Read Matthew 27 and meditate on the brokenness and suffering in the chapter.

o What did Christ's brokenness and suffering produce?

o Linger on Matthew 27:50. How does this connect to what we studied in Genesis 2 and 3?

o We have breath until God decides to return us to dust. What does this imply about the timing of the crucifixion? Give yourself time to linger in what God is teaching you.

JOURNAL OPPORTUNITY

Use the space provided to record your thoughts as you go deeper in your study.

o After studying this week, is there anything you feel prompted to surrender? Is God stirring you to take a particular action or step?

o Has feeling ordinary kept you from seeing yourself as a vessel of radiance? Can you reframe the concept of being ordinary as an opportunity to amplify the goodness of the gift of the Holy Spirit through you?

o Your story might be a lighthouse of hope for a weary traveler. Make a list of the parts of your story that seem dark but may actually be light for someone in a similar season.

Week Four Bible Verses

Mark 5:24-34

Genesis 1:31

Genesis 2:1-22

Genesis 3:19

John 20:19-22

John 7:37-39

1 Corinthians 15:45-48

2 Corinthians 12:9-12

Hebrews 5:9

2 Corinthians 4:1-10

2 Timothy 2:20-21

2 Timothy 3:14-17

2 Timothy 1:5-11

Hebrews 11:1-10

Matthew 14:13-21

Matthew 26:26-30

Matthew 27

Week Five
Redemption through a Body Broken

GOD'S BREATH brought us life, and we have the treasure of the Holy Spirit living in us. We shine the light of Christ through the cracks in our vessel, the brokenness in our story, for the sake of revealing the goodness of God despite our human errors.

Last week, we looked at the foreshadowing of Jesus breaking the bread to feed the 4,000 and breaking the bread during his last supper with the disciples. These acts of mercy were intended to be the flashing, neon arrow pointing to Golgotha, the place where Jesus was crucified. While the disciples struggled to understand, we have the benefit of stepping back and viewing this through the narrative of the entirety of scripture.

This week, we will explore how Christ's broken body becomes our eternal nourishment.

To get started, we need to return to an Old Testament story about Abraham and Isaac.

READ GENESIS 22:1–14.
Record your observations as you read.

This account has always stirred equal amounts of anxiety and relief in me. I struggle with what the Lord asks of Abraham, but I exhale an enormous sigh of relief at his provision.

The LORD Will Provide

Did you catch what Abraham named the place? *The* LORD *Will Provide.* This is the man who waited 99 years to have the child God promised and acted in obedience by taking a three-day journey when he was asked to sacrifice his son. Don't you appreciate the conversation between Abraham and Isaac in Genesis 22:7–8?

> Isaac spoke up and said to his father Abraham, "Father?"
> "Yes, my son?" Abraham replied.
> "The fire and wood are here," Isaac said, "but where
>   is the lamb for the burnt offering?"
> Abraham answered, "God himself will provide the lamb for the
>   burnt offering, my son." And the two of them went on together.

What prompted Abraham to continue walking in obedience? His faith compelled him to carry out what feels like the most heinous request anyone could ask of a father. His confidence was not in his own understanding, but in God. We see this clearly in Genesis 22:5 when Abraham told the servant "we will worship and then we will come back to you." There are only two options that explain his choice of words. He either stumbled over his words, or he was fully convinced God would provide a way out so that both he and Isaac would return.

Do you ever find yourself doubting the Lord? Do you ever feel paralyzed by doubt and fear and fail to move forward? If you are anything like me, you spend an inordinate amount of time obsessing about how a situation will be resolved.

Even though Abraham did not know how, he knew who. Knowing who he relied on compelled him to walk in obedience. Abraham's confidence reminds us to have faith, not in our own understanding or well-laid plans, but in God.

> We might not know how, but we do know who.

The Lord WILL Provide

Abraham had previously seen God's faithfulness. In Genesis 12, God called him to move from everything he knew without knowing to where God was calling him. He became a father at the age of 99. It was his faith in God's prior provision that assured him on his journey with Isaac. While we might be inclined to read this and assume he was crazy to obey, remember that he believed God would provide a sacrifice substitute for Isaac. He says to Isaac in Genesis 22:8, "God himself will provide the lamb for the burnt offering, my son." Not God might, or God could, but God *will* provide, and he did in this account.

Have you previously experienced the faithfulness of God? Like Abraham, our memories of past provision serve to bolster our complete assurance in God's current and future provision.

Let Abraham's encounter with the angel of the Lord ruminate in your mind as you consider the assurance of God's provision.

> Then he reached out his hand and took the knife to
>   slay his son. But the angel of the Lord called out
>   to him from heaven, "Abraham! Abraham!"
> "Here I am," he replied.
> "Do not lay a hand on the boy," he said. "Do not do anything
>   to him. Now I know that you fear God, because you
>   have not withheld from me your son, your only son."
> Abraham looked up and there in a thicket he saw a ram
>   caught by its horns. He went over and took the ram and
>   sacrificed it as a burnt offering instead of his son.
>
> Genesis 22:10-13

Abraham's act of obedience is interrupted—thank goodness. Abraham has the knife raised; his next act is to allow the blade to penetrate his son's flesh. Can you imagine the look of confusion on Isaac's face? Talk about a guys' trip gone terribly wrong. That moment must have included doubt, panic, betrayal, and utter sadness. I imagine the only thing giving Abraham strength to raise the knife was his faith that God would provide.

Isaac is anywhere between the ages of 12 and 30 when this event takes place. Most scholars believe he was a teenager. Imagine the reliance he had on his father, the confusion and fear in his eyes, and the panic he surely felt as his life flashed before him.

Picture Abraham's trembling hands of obedience, and his desire for the moment to be disrupted and reframed by the provision of another acceptable sacrifice. His assurance in the provision of God challenges us to examine the steadiness of our own faith. Do we trust that God will provide in our lives, homes, finances, and relationships?

> As a man thinks, so is he.

After reading and internalizing Proverbs 23:7, I extracted, adopted, and frequently repeated this phrase. As a man thinks, so is he. Because the book of Proverbs is known as Wisdom Literature, we are wise to consider how this concept plays out in our thinking and faith journey. This concept may be, in fact, the origin of Robert Merton's phrase "self-fulfilling prophecy." This theory contends that behavior influenced by our expectations causes the expectations to come true. If we doubt God's provision, we may ultimately fail to see the provision.

When we ponder God's faithfulness and rehearse his provision, our thoughts are filled with his goodness. Have you heard the saying "Thoughts become beliefs and beliefs become actions"? Put Abraham to the test with this. What was he thinking as they climbed Mt. Moriah? Maybe Abraham ruminated on this simple thought. *God will provide.* That thought, after ruminating for a portion of the journey, became a belief. How do we know? Remember what he said to the servant? "We will worship and then we will come back to you." That is confidence rooted in belief that stirred action. What action did Abraham take? He put his son on the altar and prepared to offer him as a sacrifice.

> We are wise to dwell on the faithfulness of God's provision in our lives.

The Lord Will PROVIDE

In Genesis 22:13 we read, "Abraham looked up and there in a thicket he saw a ram caught by its horns." Do you find it surprising that he looks up and suddenly sees a ram? I mean—how many bushes do you typically see at the top of a mountain? If bushes are present, are they large enough to hide a ram? The provision at that moment is supernatural and perfectly timed. Let that sink in.

Genesis 22 points to the future provision of the Lamb of God, Jesus, for the salvation of the world as illustrated in John 1:29: "Look, the Lamb of God, who takes away the sin of the world!" The ram was a substitute for Isaac, and the sacrifice of Jesus on Golgotha was a substitute for the whole world. Most of us accept that, cognitively, as fact, but I wonder how many of us let that really sink into the essence of our vessel?

Are you acquainted with the idea of scapegoating and the Day of Atonement?

Read Leviticus 16:9–10 and 16:20–22.
Record your observations as you read.

Not only was the Day of Atonement the highest holy day of the Jewish calendar, it was a day when the high priest made an atoning blood sacrifice on behalf of the sins of the people of Israel. This fulfilled the debt and penalty of sin and thus restored mankind to a right relationship with God. Following the sacrifice, a goat, symbolically carrying the sins of the people, was released into the wilderness. The process was a living illustration framing the future sacrifice of Jesus in a cultural context.

Jesus was crucified to save the world by his blood; he fulfilled the prophecy of the Old Testament and bore our sin and shame. He was called the Lamb of God because, like the ram provided for Isaac, he was the substitutionary sacrifice for us.

READ 1 JOHN 2:2, 2 CORINTHIANS 5:21, AND 1 PETER 2:23–25.
Record your observations as you read.

Considering the Day of Atonement and the scapegoat concept, these verses take on new depth of meaning. God provided for every gap that brokenness and sin created in our relationship with him. God desires that none of us would miss his provision of the gift of salvation—an act of grace extended when we were undeserving. He saw how this would play out. He was aware that he would task ordinary vessels, cracked pots if you will, to carry the gospel into the dark world. Hence the divine use of our cracks to display the light—his light.

Jesus' crucifixion fulfilled the prophecy of Isaiah 53. Although Jesus was not yet born when the prophecy of Isaiah was given, the words pointed straight to his ultimate sacrifice for the world.

Read Isaiah 53 aloud. Picture the vessel of Jesus' life crushed for us. Consider that the wounds he suffered brought us healing.

"It was the Lord's will to crush him…" Crush him. He opted to crush his son so that we could be spared the penalty of sin.

> We are hard pressed on every side, but not crushed; perplexed, but not in despair; persecuted, but not abandoned; struck down, but not destroyed. We always carry around in our body the death of Jesus, so that the life of Jesus may also be revealed in our body.
>
> 2 Corinthians 4:8–10

We are not crushed, friend. We carry the death and resurrection of Jesus with us so that our lives become a lighthouse of hope. Even when we feel like what we are facing is too much to bear, we can take comfort in knowing the same power that raised Christ from the dead dwells in us (Romans 8:11).

In his book *The Seven Habits of Highly Effective People*, Stephen R. Covey shares a story you may have heard. While battleships were out on a training, one ship captain radios with a request for another nearby ship to move out of the pathway. If the ship did not change course, the two would collide. After a few exchanges, the responding ship reveals that it is a lighthouse, so the captain who made the initial request had to set aside his pride and surrender his position. Like the captain, our egos have a unique way of complicating our surrender even when it is for our own good.[17]

The purpose of the lighthouse is to warn those at sea. The desired outcome is that a course correction is made before a devastating collision occurs, but the sailor must accept the provision of light. Are you willing to accept the Lord's provision and make necessary adjustments?

The Whole Provision

Do you suppose Abraham attempted to reject God's provision of the ram? We would think he was ridiculous if he did, right? We have the benefit of knowing that he willingly accepted the ram and completed the necessary sacrifice. In other words, he was obedient throughout the entire process.

> Being saved from our sin is only half the gospel.

As we allow our empty jars, our earthly vessels, to be filled with the light of Christ, we are invited to live a Spirit-led life. As Romans 8 teaches, this life in the Spirit is known as sanctification; the process of becoming more and more in the likeness of God is the other half of the gospel. Once we live Spirit-controlled lives, we share the light of Christ with the world. This is how the gospel advances through our—pressed but not crushed—lives.

Our lives are meant to manifest the light of Christ. The word manifest is a verb; it means to make evident, to show plainly. In what ways are you plainly showing the evidence of Christ's rescue and provision?

Jesus was broken, crushed, and put to death. We cannot settle our attention on the loss; we must remember the fulfillment and multiplication birthed from the loss. Just like the broken bread we studied, Christ's body had to be broken before the gift of salvation could be multiplied. We are reminded in 1 Peter 2:24 that "he himself bore our sins in his body on the cross, so that we might die to sins and live for righteousness; by his wounds you have been healed."

Armed with this knowledge, we are now a part of the great multiplication times table. When we see God's provision and act in obedient faith, the gospel will advance. We play our part by sharing the hope we have with the waiting world. Our waiting neighbors, worn-out children, spouses, and parents benefit from our stories of God's provision in our broken places. Are you willing to carry your message to the people closest to you and the watching world?

Consider this; "Man's extremity is God's opportunity."[18] Our seasons of extreme hurt, fear, healing, and joy are the open door to illuminate the hope of our salvation. We get to reframe our understanding of brokenness by shifting our attention from ourselves to God's provision. With one pivot, we turn from the broken cisterns we have created to the fountain of Living Water.

The Lord will provide.
He is Jehovah-jireh, our Provider.
Our redemption came through his broken body.

Read the scripture or prompt and answer the questions that follow. Give yourself time to linger in what you are learning because correct answers do not change our lives, but honest ones can.

DAY ONE

God's provision is evident in Abraham's life and in our own lives.

o Make a list of God's provisions throughout your life and in recent days.

o Contemplate the ways you have acted in obedient faith based on past provision. We are not always sure how our obedient faith impacts others for the Kingdom, but take a few moments to imagine how the gospel has advanced as a result of God's faithfulness and your obedient, active faith.

Day Two

Broken is not equivalent to unusable, but we are often led to believe that is true. Explore what God desires from us in all seasons. Read Psalm 51:17 and Isaiah 66:2.

○ What is the common thread in these two verses?

○ What strikes you about the mention of brokenness in these verses?

○ Why would such brokenness be pleasing to God?

○ How does this compel you to reframe your understanding of brokenness?

Day Three

Read Matthew 5:1–16.

○ How do these verses echo Psalm 51:17 and Isaiah 66:2 from Day Two?

○ We have a skewed perspective on the idea of being "poor." What does this really mean? Spend time studying the original meaning of the word. You can do this by visiting biblestudytools.com and searching the bible dictionary.

○ Where is your reward for obedience?

○ How does Matthew 5:14–16 encourage you as you walk out your faith?

Day Four

Read Psalms 34 slowly and record the words, phrases, or concepts that stand out to you. Read it again and answer the following questions.

o What comfort do you receive in verses 15–18?

o Verse 20 speaks of the Lord's protection through Jesus. How has Jesus' brokenness protected you?

o How can you use these verses to encourage someone walking through challenging times? Ask God to place someone on your heart who needs your encouragement, and then obediently respond.

DAY FIVE
_____

Read Psalm 116 and 2 Corinthians 4:1–18.

○ What parallels do you see in these verses?

○ What is the natural step that follows believing?

○ How does the idea of speaking and believing emerge in your day to day life?

○ End your time by reading Psalm 34 aloud.

JOURNAL OPPORTUNITY

Use the space provided to record your thoughts as you go deeper in your study.

o What have you been inspired to reframe this week? How can you retrain a familiar response?

o What is God stirring in you?

o Is there a breakthrough you have experienced this week or sometime during this study? How might your reframing or breakthrough point others to the provision of the Lord?

WEEK FIVE BIBLE VERSES

Genesis 22:1-14
Proverbs 23:7
Leviticus 16:9–10; 20-22
1 John 2:2
2 Corinthians 5:21
1 Peter 2:23–25
Isaiah 53
2 Corinthians 4:8–10
Romans 8:11
1 Peter 2:24
Psalm 51:17
Isaiah 66:2
Matthew 5:1–16
Psalm 34
Psalm 116
2 Corinthians 4:1–18

Week Six
The Great Commission:
Breaking Our Comfort Zone

Jesus' broken body was the sacrifice that paid the debt sin created and good works could not pay. His death was a substitution for our own that made a way for us and multiplied the Kingdom. It is counterintuitive to imagine that a broken spirit is something God desires of us, but this "brokenness" is not equivalent to flawed and unusable. It is about assuming a humble posture before God. This is critical to understanding and executing what we will study today: The Great Commission—a call to live from a place of rescue and restoration.

Jesus' body has been reported as missing after the crucifixion and burial. There is a story circulating about the disciples' involvement in the alleged body-snatching scandal, but the truth is they have fled to the mountain to meet with Jesus.

Read Matthew 28:11–20.

Record your observations as you read.

Consider how confusing the whole experience had been up to this point. Amid confusion and doubt, notice the posture of the disciples when they saw Jesus.

They Saw and Worshiped

Reread Matthew 28:17. The immediate response of the disciples is significant. In Matthew 28:5–10, Mary Magdalene and the other Mary encounter an angel and the resurrected Christ. They are instructed to tell the disciples to go to Galilee where they will see Jesus. Once at the mountain in Galilee, they anticipate seeing Jesus. Of course, there would be some doubt because maybe the women were overcome by sorrow and hallucinating. Can you even begin to imagine? Skepticism would seem like a reasonable response if we were in a similar circumstance.

Remember, they had not understood so much of what had happened in the weeks and days leading up to Jesus' death on the cross. Confusion and doubt surely framed the experience. And yet, pushing aside cynicism, they anticipated a reunion with Jesus.

When I am getting ready in the mornings, I listen to music. I queue up my favorite song on a particular website, hit play, and get to the pressing matters of taming the hair. If autoplay is turned on, I become so engaged in the moment that it can take me a minute to realize when the music pauses. I stop to go look at my device to figure out why the music has gone silent. Without fail, there is a question on the screen that says, "are you still watching." No. No, I am not.

It is so easy to take our eyes off one thing and focus on a lesser thing. Distraction comes in the form of all manner of good things. When the question pops up on my screen, it reminds me of a deeper spiritual truth. It is easy for me to drift into autopilot and stop actively watching for Jesus in the ordinary moments of my day, but it is critical to keep my attention focused on Jesus.

Doubt could have been enough to encourage the disciples to stop waiting for Jesus, but their expectancy kept them alert and ready

Matthew 28:17 says, "When they saw him, they worshiped him; but some doubted." The Greek word for worship in this verse is *proskuneó*: to do reverence to.[19] Because the word is a verb, we know they physically and actively worshiped on the mountain—which may have included falling prostrate to the ground.

Picture the moment. Even as tension mounted between what their physical eyes witnessed and the thoughts that must have swirled in their minds, they took a low posture. With doubt shrouding some of them, they still worshiped. There is room for our doubts in the presence of God. Let that comfort and challenge you.

Following this time of worship, the disciples were entrusted with a meaningful and specific task.

> Then Jesus came to them and said, "All authority in heaven and on earth has been given to me. Therefore go and make disciples of all nations, baptizing them in the name of the Father and of the Son and of the Holy Spirit, and teaching them to obey everything I have commanded you. And surely I am with you always, to the very end of the age."
>
> Matthew 28:18–20

Entrusted with a Task

Go. That two-letter instruction appears simple enough, but what is the cost of going? We know that Abraham was given similar instructions in Genesis 12:1. "Leave your country, your people and your father's household and go to the land I will show you." That is blind faith. He was called from, but he did not know what he was being called to. This picture of obedience is repeated in Hebrews 11:8. "By faith Abraham, when called to go to a place he would later receive as his inheritance, obeyed and went, even though he did not know where he was going." "Going" meant moving forward without a map, turn-by-turn instructions, or explanation of the big picture and ultimate goal. He had to walk away from the familiar and routine. The cost was his clarity and comfort.

> To be obedient with the instruction to go, we must marry faith with action.

Make disciples. In bible times, making disciples was not uncommon. Rabbis would make disciples by training them to become rabbis who would call students to do the same. This was the normal cycle. Jesus, who had already reminded them of the authority given to him, asked the disciples to go and share the gospel with all people. As their rabbi, Jesus gave them front row seats to the struggle that would accompany such a challenge. Crossing cultural lines, as Jesus demonstrated when he encountered the Samaritan woman, was surely a lesson in swimming upstream. Crossing gender lines, as he did with the women with the issue of blood, was new territory for making disciples of *all* people, not just the males, which was customary.

Jesus invited the disciples to push through barriers and outside their comfort zones to share what they learned under his tutelage.

Baptize. John the Baptist was the forerunner for Jesus. He was the first to emerge with the countercultural act of baptism. You may also remember that he baptized Jesus. Matthew 3:13–17 gives account to the baptism and fulfillment of the Spirit. Because Jesus fulfilled the prophecies and imparted the Holy Spirit, the disciples are equipped with full power to baptize in the name of the Father, Son, and Holy Spirit.

Teach. We would all agree that a student learns from their teacher. Part of the learning process is putting the knowledge to use in practical ways. When we practice, we commit to memory what we have seen, heard, and learned. This was the same for the disciples. They walked with Jesus, witnessed miracles, and were instructed to take what they learned, and share it with others. They were not to hoard their learning and experience.

I wonder how many of us have been guilty of holding our treasures close to our own hearts? My husband created a book of blessings for my 40th birthday, and I honestly share it with no one. He invited friends and family to write a brief account of a shared memory or affirm my value as a friend. It is a treasure to curl up with and read when I feel discouraged. The memories are personal, and the words of affirmation are intimate. They are my treasure. While I do not share the exact details of the stories and memories with the world, just seeing the book reminds me to be as generous with my encouragement as others were with me. Paying it forward is a call to let our stories of connection, healing, and hope multiply.

Have you ever heard the phrase, "you cannot give what you have not received?" Take, for instance, money. Is it possible to give money that you do not have? Impossible, right? Think about language acquisition. If you learn Spanish but never put it into practice, what happens? You slowly forget and may have trouble recalling what you would have retained with practice.

For the disciples yet doubting, they had to accept and receive the resurrection power of Christ for themselves before they could share it with others. In time, the more the mouth opened and shared, the stronger the belief. Have you ever known this to be true in your life?

If we believe that we have the treasure of the indwelling of the Spirit in jars of clay, as 2 Corinthians 4 teaches, then we remember why God would use such fragile objects to carry out his mission. The power is not from us. The call to go, baptize, and teach was prefaced by the words "all authority." The power is from God, not from us. Jesus used words that reminded the disciples that they were not being sent out powerless. They were equipped.

The disciples were to be on mission with Christ, but the invitation was for us, also.

On Mission

Have you heard of the butterfly effect? Edward Lorenz, an American meteorologist, theorized that small causes have measurable effects. His theory became a law, emphasizing how one motion of matter affects another. It is a ripple effect, in essence.

Do you see the connection between the ripple effect and the call to be on mission with Jesus? First, the disciples would be moved by Jesus, so they would then share and others would be moved, etc. The pattern would continue all the way down to us. But being "on mission" means it is not supposed to end with us. We must continue the ripple and make a decision to share the hope of the gospel with others. We cannot know the extent of our decision to share our stories and hope with others, but we can imagine when we consider how we got to where we are in our faith.

Think for a moment about who introduced you to Jesus. Once you have the image of that person, think about who may have shared Jesus with them. Follow the ripple further. Who influenced the person who influenced the person who influenced you? Do you see the power of small decisions? Now, think about a person who may have felt the ripple of our faith. Who might they influence? Do you see how this can fulfill the command to go into all nations?

> One person + one decision = maximum reach

Picture the wave in a giant stadium. There must be a willingness among the crowd to participate. This is usually spurred on by the effort of one or two people, and it is amazing to watch. If you have watched or participated, you have also seen the wave suddenly or slowly die. The crowd rises while throwing their arms up in the air, and it moves around the stadium until that section. No one stands up and the momentum dies. Being on mission means not letting the movement of the gospel end with us.

We are reminded in James 1:22 to not just be hearers of the word, but to also be doers. We may have many beliefs about what carrying out The Great Commission is supposed to look like. While different traditions of faith have ideas about how this is done correctly, I think we are wise to look to scripture to see what we can learn about "doing."

> "Therefore everyone who hears these words of mine and puts them into practice is like a wise man who built his house on the rock."
>
> Matthew 7:24

> "Now why do you call Me, 'Lord, Lord,' and do not do what I say? Everyone who comes to Me and hears My words and acts on them, I will show you whom he is like."
>
> Luke 6:46-47 NASB

> For it is not those who hear the law who are righteous in God's sight, but it is those who obey the law who will be declared righteous.
>
> Romans 2:13

Doing does not necessarily mean standing on a street corner and telling perfect strangers about Jesus. This was always my biggest concern after accepting Jesus; I imagined I would be called to a corner or a foreign land. Some will be called to such things, but I have come to understand that sharing my story or a cup of tea with a friend is also an example of being on mission.

God draws people unto himself, but we are the ones who carry the Spirit of God in our earthen vessels. We take Hope with us wherever we go.

We have many excuses for why we do not tell others about Jesus. I have reasons that range from inconvenience to fear of not having all the answers. Keep this in mind, we have the words of Hebrews 11 to speak to our list of excuses.

READ HEBREWS 11:11 AND 11:17–18. _____
Record your observations as you read.

What is your "even though"? Will you step outside your comfort zone even though you are not good at public speaking? Even though you don't have the bible memorized? Even though you aren't going onto a foreign mission field? Even though you are unsure? Even though you're single? Even though you feel afraid?

Our comfort zone quickly becomes an idol when we forget we have been entrusted with a Kingdom-sized task. We might be inclined to shrink back from anything we cannot understand or explain, or focus on our deficiencies instead of the power of the One who healed us. When we control the narrative and make excuses for why we cannot be on mission, we elevate ourselves above the call of God. Content over container theology reminds us that the power is in us, not from us. This is what compels us to share our stories.

Please don't let the concept of broken vessels get lost in this. It has not been nor will it ever be about our ability. When we take our eyes off the Lord, we become consumed with ourselves and our circumstances and get lost trying to figure it all out. The treasure is *in* us. The power comes from God and works through us. He uses willing, broken vessels.

The light of Christ shines through the whole story of our lives—the good and bad, the success and failures, the lights and darks—allowing a complete picture of the goodness of God to emerge.

Will you let him use your whole story for his glory?

Maybe he is prompting you to share the hard part of your story with a friend, coworker, neighbor, or family member. Are you willing? May we be known as people who took the Great Commission seriously—despite the cracks in our stories.

God wants to reframe our idea of brokenness to advance the gospel. He does the work through our willingness to believe that the power and provision is from him.

Think about where he may be calling you to share the hope of your healing. Who needs to witness his goodness through your story, your friendship, your authenticity?

God's power is made perfect in our weakness. You may have experiences that have chipped away at you, but those are the areas that God desires to restore and use to illuminate the power of his provision. Give him access to all the broken pieces—he has not deemed you unusable. Nothing is wasted, friend. Will you surrender the protection of your comfort zone, so the ripple of the hope of the gospel continues?

WEEK SIX REFLECTION

This is **Go** week. We have been immersed in the idea of how broken vessels serve a great purpose. We have learned that turning away from God leads to idolatry. When we are living in idolatry, we are not in tune with the Spirit because we are consumed with ourselves. Spend time this week praying about your willingness to reframe past or current seasons of brokenness, your assurance in God's ability to provide, and potential steps outside your comfort zone you feel compelled to take. Make a list of avenues he has opened for you to share your faith. Is there a particular part of your story you sense he wants to use? Make a list of people for whom you can begin praying to receive the rescue and restoration of Jesus.

JOURNAL OPPORTUNITY

Use the space provided to record your thoughts as you go deeper in your study.

o What have you allowed the Lord to reframe during this study?

o How are you different now than when you first started this study?

o Write down thoughts and ideas he brings about your next steps as you spend time in prayer and quiet reflection.

Week Six Bible Verses

Matthew 28:5–20

Genesis 12:1

Hebrews 11:8

Matthew 3:13–17

2 Corinthians 4

James 1:22

Matthew 7:24

Luke 6:46-47

Romans 2:13

Hebrews 11:11, 17–18

12   Dr. Ray Pritchard, "The Woman at the Well : Christ Speaks to the Problem of a Guilty Past," Sermons, Keep Believing Ministries, January 14, 2001, www.keepbelieving.com/sermon/the-woman-at-the-well-christ-speaks-to-the-problem-of-a-guilty-past/.

13   Allison Lim, "Ancient Story, Modern Message: The Cracked Pot," Blog, TCM World, August 14, 2020, www.tcmworld.org/ancient-story-modern-message-the-cracked-pot/.

14   Craig S. Keener, *Matthew*, The IVP New Testament Commentary Series 1 (Downers Grove, IL: InterVarsity Press, 1997), 193.

15   Debbie McDaniel, "How to Find Beauty in Brokenness," Faith, Crosswalk.com, January 22, 2015, http://www.crosswalk.com/faith/women/how-to-find-beauty-in-brokenness.html.

16   "St. Mother Teresa Quotes on Prayer," Vatican Site, May 14, 2017, https://www.vaticansite.com/st-mother-teresa-quotes-prayer/.

17   Stephen R. Covey. *The Seven Habits of Highly Effective People*. (Switzerland: Free Press, 2004), 33.

18   Bible Study Tools, s.v. "Jehovah-Jireh," https://www.biblestudytools.com/dictionary/jehovah-jireh/.

19   "Strong's Exhaustive Concordance," Bible Hub, s.v "4352. proskuneó," https://www.google.com/url?q=https://biblehub.com/greek/4352.htm&sa=D&-source=editors&ust=1631326073484000&usg=AOvVaw09ufRHi-SE-Qf7s7QaAY8Mw.

About the Author

Alyssa DeLosSantos is a writer, speaker, podcaster, and founder of the #Sowkind Movement. She is passionate about hope, truth, and restoration and loves encouraging others to lean into the fullness of who they were created to be. She believes every scar is a storyline that leads to connection and community, so she routinely shares her journey through broken seasons and the treasures she excavated along the way.

Alyssa lives in South Texas with her husband, three children, and one highly codependent furry friend. She loves cheering for her people, eating chips and queso, sipping a London Fog, and going on adventures in her vintage VW van.

Alyssa is a contributing author for *A Moment to Breathe: 365 Devotions That Meet You in Your Everyday Mess*, and her ebook, *Wisdom in the Weeds*, captures the heart of her journey through fear. You can find more of her work at www.alyssadelossantos.com.